London Midland Region

THE **CHANGING RAILWAY** SCENE

London Midland Region

DEREK HUNTRISS

Ian Allan
PUBLISHING

Dedication

To my partner Elaine Simmons and to my mother Mabel, for being prepared to give me the time and space to research, design and write this title — a heartfelt Thank You.

Acknowledgements

I would like to take this opportunity to thank the following people for their generous contribution of time and knowledge in the preparation and checking of this title.

To John Edgington, former member of the library staff at the National Railway Museum, for sharing his in-depth knowledge of British railway history with additional anecdotal information in the captioning of the pictures used and for reading and checking the final page proofs. To Neville Simms of Coventry, a lifelong friend and RCTS member, for checking the manuscript and those of my previous efforts, also for correcting and filling in the gaps in the work.

Finally I would like to thank Martin Welch, retired British Railways Civil Engineering Manager, for writing the Foreword for this somewhat extensive subject and for checking the rest of the manuscript.

As always deepest thanks are offered to all the photographers whose work is included in these pages. Without their efforts in recording the railway scene over the past 50 years this title could not have been contemplated.

Bibliography

Hugh Ballantyne: *The Colour of British Rail — Vol 2 West Coast Main Line;* Atlantic Transport Publishing
Colin Boocock: *British Railways in Colour 1948-1968;* Ian Allan
W. Philip Connolly: *British Railways Pre-Grouping Atlas and Gazetteer;* Ian Allan
H. G. Forsythe: *Men of the Diesels;* Atlantic Transport Publishing
Peter Fox: *The Midland Line in Sheffield;* Platform 5
C. J. Gammell: *LMS Branch Lines;* GRQ Publications
Derek Huntriss: *The LMS Pacifics — Vol 6;* Atlantic Transport Publishing
Derek Huntriss: *London Midland in the Fells — Vol 5;* Atlantic Transport Publishing
L. A. Nixon: *BR Colour Album;* Ian Allan
Brian Sharpe: *British Railways — Modernisation to Privatisation;* Mortons Media Group
Robert Stephens: *Diesel Pioneers;* Atlantic Transport Publishing
British Rail — Main Line Gradient Profiles; Ian Allan
Other Publications: *Backtrack, Modern Railways, Railway Magazine, Railway World, Steam Days, Traction Magazine, Trains Illustrated, History of Railways, Great Trains, The World of Trains, RCTS Railway Observer.*

Derek Huntriss
Sandiacre and Coventry
March 2008

Half-title page: **Before full electrification on the LM West Coast main line between Weaver Junction and Glasgow principal services were in the hands of the 50 English Electric D400 Co-Co Type 5s. Here Nos D403 and D406 power an up express past Farington Curve Junction on 13 July 1971.** *Peter Fitton*

Title page: **With overhead electrification already in place, recently ex-works Britannia Pacific No 70047 waits to take over an up express at Crewe in April 1960. This standard design had abandoned the traditional 6ft 6in-6ft 9in coupled wheels in favour of a diameter of 6ft 2in used on the LNER's 'V2s' yet the overall styling suggested a strong London Midland & Scottish influence.** *Martin S. Welch*

Front cover:
Having taking over the southbound 'Thames-Clyde Express' in Leeds, Kentish Town (14B's) 'Jubilee' 4-6-0 No 45649 *Hawkins* climbs away from Sheffield Midland near Millhouses in May 1959.
Derek Penny

Rear cover, top:
The transitional scene on the Banbury branch at Buckingham on 24 August 1956 as No 79901 has arrived as the 1.30pm from Banbury whilst Standard Class 2 2-6-2T No 84002 waits to depart as the push-pull working for Bletchley. This operation required the passengers to change trains together with the contents of the guards van. *John Edgington*

Rear cover, bottom:
This picture, taken at Crewe District Electric Depot on 12 August 1960, shows GEC/NBL 3,300 Class AL4 No E3038 which had entered service some two months earlier. This 10-strong class built in 1960-61 had a high failure rate, temperamental mercury-arc rectifiers being only partially cured by expensive modifications. *Martin S. Welch*

First published 2008

ISBN 978 0 7110 3243 9

Published by Ian Allan Publishing Ltd, Hersham, Surrey KT12 4RG.
Printed in England by Ian Allan Printing Ltd, Hersham, Surrey KT12 4RG.

Code: 0806/C1

Visit the Ian Allan Publishing website at:
www.ianallanpublishing.com

Contents

This October 1969 picture shows Brush-Sulzer 2,750hp Co-Co Type 4 No D1799 working a special merry-go-round test train past Welbeck Colliery Junction towards Clipstone. Merry-go-round operation was conceived initially as the continuous operation of block trains between colliery and power station that would be loaded and unloaded while moving slowly under or over storage hoppers. *Cliff Woodhead*

Foreword

None can halt the march of progress. Improve or die — such is life. In all of man's endeavours it is so, and the railway is no exception. During the two decades from 1955 to 1975, the London Midland Region experienced a considerable transformation in all of its business and resources. Primarily there were tremendous changes in motive power and equipment.

As the first day of 1948 dawned, the 'Big Four' companies were combined into a new entity, named simply as 'British Railways'. The old company Boards of Directors became Regional Boards to manage their own regions, and reported to the British Transport Commission (BTC), later BR Board, at its headquarters at Marylebone in the old Great Central Railway Hotel. The BR Board was supported by HQ Departmental Officers, who maintained standardisation, and chaired the key policy committees on which the regional representatives sat.

Whilst the old company workshops continued to produce new steam engines to the old designs, it was realised that up-to-date designs would be needed. In 1948 a series of locomotive exchanges were arranged where various examples of current motive power were tested on the same routes, side by side, to assess where further development would be productive within the design of the new generation of steam locomotives.

In the meantime Crewe and Horwich continued to build LMS-design 'Black Fives' until 1949, some of these locomotives having modern refinements such as Caprotti valve gear, double chimneys and roller bearings. Other types, such as the Fairburn 2-6-4T engines, were also perpetuated well into BR days. Other classes, such as the 'Royal Scots', continued to be rebuilt.

The BR Standard designs were farmed out to the various Chief Mechanical & Electrical Engineers (CM & EE) Drawing offices. The LMR found itself dealing with the Pacifics, and by 1951 the 'Britannia' class were emerging from Crewe Works, No 70004 *William Shakespeare* going on display at the Festival of Britain Exhibition in London in that year. Other designs quickly followed and became familiar sights throughout the network. Whilst some of the old hands thought the performances of the new engines to be inferior to their Old Company predecessors, at least the newer locomotives were much easier to maintain. Their lives, however, were to be rather short. This was in part due to the poor estimated efficiency of the steam locomotive at 15%, compared to that of diesel at 55% and electric at 90%.

By 1954 it was realised that significant reinvestment was essential and in 1955 the 'Modernisation Plan' was announced. On the LMR this entailed complete replacement of steam motive power over the following 15 years by main line diesel locomotives and multiple-unit railcars, except for the West Coast main lines which were to be electrified. The WCML traffic levels were such that the considerable cost of overhead line electrification at 25kV ac was estimated to bring a sufficient financial return to satisfy Whitehall investment rules. A pilot scheme was undertaken on the Styal line, followed by the Crewe to Manchester route which was completed in September 1960. Crewe to Liverpool followed on 1 January 1962, while Crewe to Stafford was switched on in late 1962, and thence to Rugby in 1964. London was reached by 1966 and the Birmingham area completed in 1967. Besides the overhead electrical equipment work, there was considerable resignalling work undertaken, including the introduction of power boxes. Many bridges had to be rebuilt, and main stations such as Euston, Manchester, Birmingham New Street and Stafford were completely rebuilt. A new north flyover at Rugby was built saving some 40 express train conflictions. New electric motive power maintenance depots were built together with electric feeder stations and control rooms. Automatic warning systems were installed throughout.

Speeds of 100mph were to be catered for, so that considerable track improvement was needed, large capital sums were expended on realignment work and reballasting. Continuous welded rail was installed extensively. Initially on the Styal line the ex-WR gas turbine, No 18100, was converted to an electric locomotive No E1000, which was used for driver training. A hundred locomotives were ordered originally from various manufacturers followed by a further 100 for the extension to Euston. Also ordered were some 45 four-car electric multiple-units for local services (Class AM4).

They were built at Wolverton with Associated Electrical Industries (AEI) equipment. A further 50 four-car electric multiple-units (Class AM10) were built at Derby.

By 1959 the motorway age was dawning with the opening of the first section of the M1. The second part of the WCML electrification from Weaver Junction to Glasgow was urgently needed to meet the growing competition from road and air alternatives. BR wanted to follow on straight away with this part of the scheme but it was not to be until 1970 that the government would give the go-ahead. The first electric train ran through to Glasgow on 6 May 1973. For this final phase, a further 36 (Class 87) locomotives were built at Crewe.

Under the 1955 Modernisation Plan, 171 prototype diesel locomotives were ordered from various manufacturers. The LMS, besides producing diesel shunters, was building in 1947 a pair of main line diesels (Nos 10000 and 10001), to compare with the last two steam Pacifics, Nos 46256 and 46257. So it was logical to select Derby to develop the 'Peak' Type 4 (1Co-Co1), later Class 44, based on the experiences of the performance of 10000/10001 and also those of the Bulleid-design diesels Nos 10201/2/3, also 1Co-Co1 wheel arrangement, which had come from the Southern to the LM in 1955. Ten 'Peaks' were built with Sulzer engines capable of delivering 2,300hp, emerging from Derby Works in 1959, each unit weighing a hefty 133 tons, hence the extra pony wheel axles. The first diesel locomotives built at Derby, however, were twenty of the Type 2 Bo-Bo (D5000 series — later Class 24), also with Sulzer engines, these commencing work in 1958. Earlier the LMR had received a few Bo-Bo Type 1s (later Class 20s) built by English Electric at the Vulcan Foundry in 1957. A year later came the Metrovick Co-Bos (D5700 series) fitted with Crossley engines. The 20 engines were allocated to Derby for work on the Midland Lines. Famously they were diagrammed to work in pairs on the 'Condor' container overnight fast freight services between London and Glasgow, and also on some Manchester to London express services. Unreliability and high maintenance problems resulted in them being banished to Northwest England in a reduced role and all were withdrawn when barely 10 years old.

The first 10 English Electric 2,000hp Type 4 1Co-Co1 (later Class 40) locomotives from Vulcan Foundry were allocated to the Eastern Region, but more were ordered in due course, and in 1959 these began to take over the WCML expresses from steam traction, as a stopgap until electrification. Meanwhile the 'Peak' design was uprated to 2,500hp and new locomotives (Class 45) were built in quantity to take over express services on the Midland main line.

A most successful all-round Type 4 Co-Co diesel locomotive (later Class 47) was introduced, being built from 1962 by Brush and BR at Crewe. Whilst most of them went to other regions, the LMR received some a couple of years later at Crewe North and on the Nottingham Division.

Some time earlier in 1955, English Electric had built the prototype *Deltic* (DP1) which produced 3,300bhp using Napier marine delta-form engines. This unique locomotive in its distinctive light blue livery was intensively tested on the LMR, and eventually led to an order for a production run of 22 examples for high-speed services on the East Coast main line. A little later English Electric built a prototype Gas Turbine locomotive, GT3, which was also tested on the LM but the design was not thought practical and was not pursued. More successful was a further prototype, DP2, which emerged from the Vulcan Foundry in 1962. The locomotive, equipped with a new design of 2,700hp engine, after testing again on the LMR, led to the order for 50 examples. They had Co-Co type bogies and were built in 1967 and 1968 to work in multiple on Scottish services north of Crewe prior to electrification of these routes, so providing adequate power over Shap and Beattock with higher speeds. At full electrification the class was transferred to the Western Region as Class 50.

About this period Vulcan Foundry was busy building English Electric Type 3 Co-Cos (Class 37) locomotives for other regions. Meanwhile Derby Works continued to turn out the Sulzer Class 24 and 25 diesels primarily for the Midland Lines.

Diesel multiple-units were built in large numbers, Derby Works producing examples from 1955, but many good designs came from private manufacturers. Savings on manning and more productive diagrams resulted, and they rapidly took over most semi-fast and local passenger trains from steam traction.

Most types of electric and diesel locomotives were used on freight services as well as passenger, but when the heavier 'block' freight trains came along, more modern powerful engines were developed.

The Midland Pullman units were introduced between St Pancras and Manchester in 1960 to provide an alternative First class business service while the WCML suffered delays due to electrification works. These trains in turn led to the introduction of the High Speed Trains which are still widely operating on the Midland Route.

The London Midland of today seems very different to its previous character in the days of steam. Derek Huntriss is to be congratulated for assembling this fascinating collection of classic and historic colour images showing so vividly the early period of change from steam to modern traction on the London Midland.

Martin S. Welch   March 2008

Top: **Newly-constructed Brush-Sulzer Type 4 No D1606 is depicted under the catenary at Crewe in August 1964. The first member of this class No D1500 had made its debut on 6 September 1962 when it travelled from the Brush Locomotive Works to Crewe for weighing.** *Martin S. Welch*

Above: **A classic action study of rebuilt 'Royal Scot' No 46108** *Seaforth Highlander* **as it heads north from Lancaster in June 1962. Allocated to Carlisle Upperby (12B) Motive Power Depot (MPD) in November 1960 it was withdrawn from there in December 1962.** *Derek Penney*

Another fine study taken north of Lancaster in June 1962. Here Carlisle Upperby's (12B) rebuilt 'Patriot' No 45532 *Illustrious* heads a northbound express. Having just been allocated to Upperby that month, No 45532 remained in traffic until February 1964. *Derek Penney*

An immaculate No 46228 *Duchess of Rutland* at Crewe in August 1958, waiting to take the up 'Midday Scot' to Euston. Electrification was then well under way; after three years' work, Stage 1 of the London Midland Region's 25kV electrification was completed with the inauguration of electric traction between Crewe and Manchester, via both routes — Styal and Stockport — commencing on 12 September 1960.
Martin S. Welch

Taken from inside the electric maintenance depot at Crewe on 12 August 1960, this picture shows a brand new EMU which had arrived for crew training for the Manchester to Crewe route. At this date the depot was still under construction as can be seen with the partially completed steps to the inspection pit. *Martin S. Welch*

1

West Coast Transition

The British Transport Commission's decision to electrify the former LNWR main line between Euston and Glasgow was one of the most ambitious projects envisaged in the 1955 Modernisation Plan. For the replacement of steam traction whilst introducing diesel motive power, British industry was able to provide relatively limited expertise gained mainly from export contracts and foreign licence agreements, but for main line 25kV electrification there was no previous experience.

Electrification of the 401 route miles took place between 1962 and 1974. Planning and survey work began in 1957 and followed the decision to use the overhead 25kV system, an entirely new concept on BR. This equipment was tested on the line between Slade Green Junction and Wilmslow on the Styal line south of Manchester in 1958.

The first section to be opened was that between Manchester and Crewe, services commencing in September 1960. This was followed in January 1962 by the section between Crewe and Liverpool. On the WCML electric services began between Crewe and Stafford in January 1963, extending southwards to Nuneaton in March 1964 and Rugby in November of that year. North of the border in Scotland, the line from Motherwell to Glasgow Central was inaugurated in May 1962, this being part of the overall plan for the electrification of the Glasgow area.

The final section of the electrification between Manchester, Liverpool and London — from Queens Park into Euston station —was energised at 25kV for testing on 25 October 1965. After completion of this programme the first train from Euston electrically hauled, by Class AL6 Bo-Bo locomotive No E3171, was the 08.35 to Liverpool on Monday 22 November. Early workings of the new outer-suburban stock on the inaugural day were the 07.30 from Tring and the 06.59 from Northampton.

By 1970 the project to complete the remainder of the WCML had begun. To maintain the scheduled services, albeit with diversions and retimings, this meant that the main line from Weaver Junction, north of Crewe to Glasgow, took four years to complete, through Anglo-Scottish services commencing on 6 May 1974.

Four manufacturers had built what became Classes 81-84, each using electrical equipment from a different supplier. These locomotives proved somewhat unreliable and were rebuilt in the 1970s. The Class 85 locomotives, built in BR's own workshops, were a significant improvement of the earlier classes, but with the impending completion of the London and Manchester/Liverpool electrification in 1966, 100 Class 86 locomotives were ordered. This class was intended to use all of the best features of the Class 85, but in an effort to reduce costs the frame-mounted motors were replaced in favour of the simpler nose-suspended motors.

With hindsight this exercise led to an increase in general track damage and a poorer ride for the passengers and only a very expensive modification programme made the Class 86 generally acceptable.

For the lines north of Crewe with the steep climbs over Shap and Beattock, a more powerful type of locomotive was required. The 36 Class 87s with a continuous rating of 5,000hp compared with the 4,400hp of the Class 86 were designed by BR, and built by its subsidiary British Rail Engineering Limited (BREL). In general the design of this class closely resembled that of its predecessors, but the '87s' could be clearly identified by having two cab windows instead of three.

In service the Class 87 proved to be an excellent machine, but cases of rough riding were cured by the fitting of horizontal yaw dampers to the bogies. A second series of Class 87s was ordered in 1986, but owing to major developments with electric traction equipment, they were designated Class 90 before construction had commenced.

Forty years later the once state-of-the-art electrical track and signalling installations were virtually life-expired and required massive investment to upgrade Britain's busiest main line, with all of the disruption that again entailed. One surprising statistic is that a high proportion of WCML freight and passenger traffic today is in the hands of diesel motive power, proving that it is uneconomic and inconvenient to change motive power once or even twice on long-distance services.

Right: **The transition from steam to diesel motive power is seen here at the old Euston terminus prior to its complete rebuilding. This picture shows an unidentified English Electric Type 4 (Class 40) alongside rebuilt 'Royal Scot' 4-6-0 No 46155 *The Lancer* at Platforms 2 and 1 respectively.** *John Edgington*

Above: **Class AL6 electric No E3142 is seen leaving the rebuilt Euston station in May 1968. Introduced in 1965, the styling of this class was similar to the five prototypes, but there were technical changes based on operating experience with the earlier locomotives. The axle-hung motors on this class severely punished the track — and the drivers — at speed. The fitting of flexicoil springs and resilient wheels, in which rubber blocks took half the motor weight, made Class AL6 a valuable member of the BR electric locomotive fleet.** *Ray Reed*

Left: **Another view taken inside the old Euston station, this time depicting Willesden (1A) MPD's rebuilt 'Royal Scot' No 46126 *Royal Army Service Corps* which has arrived at Platform 2. No 46126 was to see out its days on Great Central metals working out of Annesley (16D) MPD before being withdrawn in September 1963.** *Cliff Woodhead*

Above: '**Coronation**' **class Pacific No 46252** *City of Leicester* **is seen at Kilburn on 18 August 1962 as it works the 11.35am Euston to Windermere. No 6252 (with 6232) were the first 'Coronations' to be fitted with smoke deflectors, in 1945, No 6253 and subsequent engines carrying them from new.** *John Carter*

Below: **No 46240** *City of Coventry* **threads the north London suburbs as it heads a down train of mainly LMS stock near Kensal Green. Along with Nos 46239, 46245 and 41239, No 46240 was one of the last locomotives to leave Camden depot when it closed to steam on 9 September 1963, working out its days from Willesden (1A) MPD.** *John Carter*

Above: With the former LMS Stonebridge Park power station clearly visible above the rear of the train 'Coronation' class Pacific No 46248 *City of Leeds* is seen crossing the third-rail Euston to Watford electric lines with a northbound express. *John Carter*

Below: Having crossed to the down side of the main lines near Stonebridge Park, the Euston to Watford third-rail electric lines are in the foreground of this picture taken near Hatch End showing rebuilt 'Royal Scot' 4-6-0 No 46165 *The Ranger (12th London Regiment)* as it works a late afternoon departure from Euston. *John Carter*

Above: **Another late afternoon departure from Euston is captured near Hatch End, this time behind a very begrimed 'Princess Royal' No 46206 *Princess Marie Louise*. At a very late stage in its career No 46206 was paired with a tender having a steam-operated coal pusher to enable it to work under the overhead catenary.** *John Carter*

Below: **At Hatch End the now preserved 'Coronation' class Pacific No 46233 *Duchess of Sutherland* works the down 'Merseyside Express'. Following preservation at Butlin's Heads of Ayr holiday camp and subsequent restoration at Bressingham Steam Museum, No 46233 is today actively used on main line tours based at the Midland Railway — Butterley.** *John Carter*

Top: **With a train from the south coast to the West Midlands, 'Jubilee' 4-6-0 No 45554 *Ontario* passes under the partially constructed catenary at Hillmorton on 17 August 1963. Above the locomotive is the signal on the 'new' (1881) line from Northampton.** *N. Simms*

Bottom: **On 26 October 1963 ex-Crosti-boilered '9F' 2-10-0 No 92020 is depicted as it speeds a southbound freight through Rugby whilst 'Britannia' Pacific No 70024 *Vulcan* is departing with a down semi-fast.** *Bryan Hicks*

Above: **At the north end of Rugby station three '8F' 2-8-0s and an Ivatt Class 2MT 2-6-0 travel light engine to Rugby MPD on 9 September 1963. It is interesting to note that the 'going home' hooter at the adjacent AEI factory was the whistle retrieved from the old Cunard ocean liner RMS *Mauretania*.** *Bryan Hicks*

Below: **Parked against the former LNWR goods depot at Coventry is AEI/Birmingham Railway Carriage & Wagon Works Class AL1 electric No E3020. The electrification of the West Coast main line from Manchester to Euston had been opened in stages, the current being switched on from Birmingham to Coventry on 15 August 1966.** *Ray Reed*

Left: **English Electric Type 4 No D344 is seen under the wires between Rugby and Nuneaton at Brinklow on 16 March 1963 as it heads 1A25 — an up Llandudno–Euston passenger working. The photographer recalls his disappointment at that time as this diagram was regularly booked for steam haulage. Only months later, on 8 August, the single most publicised event involving a member of this class took place at Sears Green when the up Glasgow mail was stopped by a masked gang who proceeded to rob the train of an estimated £2,500,000.** *N. Simms*

Left: **'Coronation' class Pacific No 46225 *Duchess of Gloucester* heads a Glasgow to London parcels at Brinklow on 16 March 1963. This working was also another good bet for steam haulage at this time although booked for an English Electric Type 4.** *N. Simms*

Below: **Newly delivered 'AL1s' Nos E3021 and E3015 stand outside Crewe District Electric Depot in 1960. Introduced that year, the first BR ac electrics were painted in the distinctive electric blue and travelling at speeds of up to 100mph they represented the ultimate image of the modern railway.** *Ray Reed*

Super power for the up 'Red Rose' as it leaves Crewe behind No 46256
Sir William A. Stanier F.R.S. and 'Royal Scot' No 46164 *The Artists'*
Rifleman on 15 August 1958. The reason for the 'Scot' being used on a
Friday was for it to return with an additional service to Liverpool on
the Saturday. *Martin S. Welch*

Right: **Patricroft (9H) MPD's 'Jubilee' No 45600 *Bermuda* has been relegated to freight duties as it is seen heading a southbound freight north of Euxton Junction in August 1964. A Patricroft locomotive for much of its working life, No 45600 was transferred to Newton Heath (9D) MPD in January 1965, withdrawal being in December of that year.** *Derek Penney*

Above: **Repainted to work a King's Cross–Doncaster railtour on 9 June 1963, No 46245 *City of London* is seen two weeks later on 22 June as it heads the down 'Lakes Express' north of Preston. No 46245 was named by Sir Samuel G. Joseph in a ceremony at Euston station on 20 July 1943.** *Peter J. Fitton*

Left: **Nine years after the first of the class made its debut on BR, Brush-Sulzer Type 4 No 1838 heads north over Shap with a down express on 17 July 1971. December 1967 had seen the end of regular steam working over Shap.** *Peter J. Fitton*

22

Above: **Stanier 'Coronation' Pacific No 46248 *City of Leeds* is waiting for an extra coach to be added at Carlisle as it works a relief to the 'Midday Scot' on 10 August 1962. With only three through platforms at this station there was always a headache for the operating department with reliefs to many of the Anglo-Scottish expresses.** *N. Simms*

Below: **Formally withdrawn from traffic on 12 October 1964, No 46256 *Sir William A. Stanier F.R.S.* was reinstated to work the RCTS 'Scottish Lowlander' railtour on 26 October 1964. Pictured here alongside Carlisle No 4 signalbox, No 46256 had just completed the first northbound leg.** *N. Fields*

Prior to the mass introduction of 'Peaks' to Midland Line passenger services, Kentish Town (14B's) 'Jubilee' 4-6-0 No 45649 *Hawkins* is in charge of the up 'Thames-Clyde Express' as it climbs away from Sheffield near Millhouses in May 1959. No 45649 is coming up on the Manchester line, the London line being switched out for engineering work. *Derek Penney*

2
Modernising the Midland

Despite pursuing a relatively conservative policy in motive power some unusual designs have emerged from Derby, the locomotive headquarters of the old Midland Railway. In the dawn of the diesel era there was the very interesting Fell locomotive based on a pair of diesel engines at each end of a chassis mounted over undriven bogies and mechanically connected to several central pairs of driving wheels.

As early as 1942, Derby produced detailed plans for a 1,600bhp A1A-A1A and also a 1A-Bo-A1 of similar power.

When it became clear that the days of steam were numbered, main line diesel traction appeared on the Midland by 1958/9 in the form of the unusual Metropolitan-Vickers Co-Bo Type 2 design which was used for working the 'Condor' freight between Hendon and Gushetfaulds Yard, Glasgow. These Type 2s were not a success, but with diagrammed mileages of over 500 they afforded a valuable background of experience with diesel traction before the advent of the Type 4s.

When the Planning Section of the LMR decided to eliminate steam from the Midland Division late in 1957 the replacement for long-distance passenger workings was ordered as 122 Type 4 locomotives to be constructed under the 1960 Building Programme. Always associated with their Midland Line duties, the introduction of the 'Peaks' enabled the Manchester services to be dieselised by February 1961. It is perhaps true to say that no other network of main lines needed diesel traction more than the Midland.

With the introduction of diesel traction to Midland Line services was the problem of how to make best economical use of the remaining steam locomotives, in particular the more modern LMS and BR designs displaced from the principal diagrams. The first move came early in 1961 with the displacement of most of the 'Royal Scots' from passenger work at Kentish Town, Nottingham and Trafford Park. This move was followed later in the year by elimination of 'Jubilees' from other principal main line depots. Further redistribution was needed by the summer of 1962 when the Class 5 and BR Class 4 4-6-0s made redundant could be employed better elsewhere in addition to growing numbers of displaced 2-8-0s and 2-10-0

freight locomotives. Therefore in September 1962 most of the 'Jubilees' at Burton-on-Trent and all the 'B1' 4-6-0s at Woodford Halse were replaced by Class 5 4-6-0s and 2-10-0s were put to much of the work previously undertaken by Class 8F 2-8-0s; this move made possible the transfer of 22 Class 8F engines to Annesley to eliminate the former LNER Class O1 2-8-0s there.

With the closure of Neasden depot the problem arose of dividing the BR Class 4 2-6-0s from the LMS-built examples which, whilst being equivalent for operational purposes, created different issues from the stores point of view. The majority of Neasden's BR 2-6-0s were fitted with tripcocks for working over the Metropolitan and GC lines and had hitherto been confined to Cricklewood: the LMS type were transferred to Heaton Mersey and Trafford Park in exchange for BR Standard locomotives. Neasden's remaining 2-6-0s were sent to Woodford Halse and made possible the withdrawal of that depot's three Class J39 0-6-0s.

Whilst this could appear to be an unnecessary series of mass transfers it was in fact a carefully planned redistribution of motive power to make the best use of not only the new diesel locomotives but particularly the remaining steam power on the Midland Lines.

In 1966 the Midland Lines were to get the 'Best-Ever' services when a completely revised timetable was introduced on 18 April. By providing fast, frequent and regular services between London, the East Midlands and the North, and between principal towns *en route* it was hoped to stimulate traffic even if trains were not filled initially. There were seven more services in each direction which was achieved with about two-thirds of the stock previously required. Cleaning and servicing of carriages at the termini gave an average turn-round time of 45min and there was more intensive use of diesel motive power.

The service of trains between North-East England and South Wales and the West of England via Birmingham New Street offered better journey times in many cases. Other benefits of the timetable were faster journeys for Luton and Bedford travellers and a completely revised Sunday service; and more trains with restaurant and buffet car facilities.

Above: **With Mill Hill Broadway station in the background the 'Midland Pullman' set forms the down evening service to Manchester leaving St Pancras at 6.10pm. Between trips from Manchester the set was employed on an additional trip to Leicester. This First-class-only service which commenced running on 4 July 1960 was operated by two six-car sets, one being used as standby, both being serviced and stabled at Reddish electric depot in Manchester. With the completion of the Euston to Manchester electrification in 1966 with alternative Pullman services, both sets were transferred to the Western Region.** *Colour-Rail*

Left: **Taken from Great Northern House this picture shows the Midland Railway's St Pancras station in 1960. Changes made in 1963 included the repainting of the roof in a light stone colour, a 9ft platform barrier screen was erected, the passenger concourse was enlarged, and the cab approach road between Platforms 5 and 6 was closed.** *Cliff Woodhead*

Above: **Transferred from Leeds Holbeck (55A) MPD to Kentish Town (14B) MPD in December 1958 'Royal Scot' 4-6-0 No 46133 *The Green Howards* speeds an express through the platform on the down fast at Mill Hill in August 1960.** *John Carter*

Below: **Seen on the Midland main line near Houghton Conquest signalbox, south of Bedford, 'Peak' No D66 heads an up express in September 1966. Dieselisation of the Manchester services had been virtually completed by February 1961.** *Derek Penney*

Top: **Crosti-boilered '9F' 2-10-0 No 92028 prepares an up coal train for Brent Sidings at Finedon Road near Wellingborough on 16 July 1959. Of 36 '9F' 2-10-0s allocated to Wellingborough shed 10 were fitted with Crosti boilers and with the limitation of operating diagrams these locomotives only achieved between 600 and 700 miles per week.**
Ken Fairey

Above: **Crewe-built 'Peak' No D96 is seen outside the depot at Kettering in August 1963. The four-character headcode system was introduced in 1961 and replaced the disc and electric light headcodes on the prototypes. In addition to their duties on the Midland main line the class were regular performers on north-east to south-west services.**
Martin S. Welch

Above: **Showing a strange headlamp code for an express, 'Jubilee' 4-6-0 No 45648** *Wemyss* **is seen passing Gloucester Tramway Crossing with a northbound working on 20 October 1962.** *N. Simms*

Below: **On 20 October 1962 Coalville (15D) MPD's '4F' 0-6-0 No 44279 passes Gloucester Tramway Crossing with a southbound train of tank wagons.** *N. Simms*

One of 21 'Jubilee' 4-6-0s nominally allocated to Burton (17B) MPD in 1962, No 45648 *Wemyss*, somewhat lacking its former pristine condition, is depicted on 25 August. Displaced from their main line duties they replaced the ageing Hughes-Fowler 2-6-0 'Crabs' and were used on beer trains. *Ken Fairey*

Right: **With fully finished two-tone green Brush-Sulzer Type 4 No D1579 in the background, sister locomotive No D1751 is seen in a pink primer at Derby (17A) MPD on 28 June 1964.** *T. B. Owen*

Above: **Trent, near Derby, was a station surrounded by fields, without main road access. It was intriguing for the timetable connoisseur as two trains departing from both sides of the island platform might both be bound for St Pancras. Built in 1862 Trent station was built as an interchange and on peak days it handled more trains than Nottingham Midland and Victoria combined. As the Beeching cuts of the 1960s bit deeply into rail services it was on 1 January 1968 at 00.01 that the last train departed. The fine array of Midland semaphores is evident in this picture taken on 22 August 1959.** *Ken Fairey*

Right: **The final development of the Midland 0-6-0 locomotives was in the shape of a superheated Class 4 variety. It can be claimed that all of the 1,761 engines constructed over a period of 65 years stem from Johnson's original design of 1875. Here Class 4F No 43854 arrives at Coalville with coal empties in September 1963.** *Geoff Rixon*

Below: **This view taken at Ambergate on 27 May 1961 shows 'Peak' No D23 passing with the up 'Palatine' express from Manchester to St Pancras. Ambergate was a fascinating triangular junction between the famous Peak Forest route to Manchester and the Midland main line north to Chesterfield. Direct running off the Peak Forest route in a northbound direction was possible via Ambergate West and East Junctions.** *Cliff Woodhead*

Bottom: **The 'Peaks' were in their outward style surprisingly like that of the pioneer LMS main line diesels Nos 10000-1. The pilot scheme locomotives were pretty soon confined to freight workings from Toton, but the rest rapidly took over the workings previously associated with the 'Royal Scots' and 'Jubilees'. Here No D165 is arriving at Matlock Bath with a Derby to Manchester stopping train on 16 June 1962.** *Cliff Woodhead*

Above: In this picture taken at Millers Dale on 24 June 1961 unrebuilt 'Patriot' No 45509 *The Derbyshire Yeomanry* works an up train whilst an unidentified tender-first '4F' 0-6-0 has charge of an up goods. The tender attached to this locomotive has extended side plates to cover the coal when used on snowplough duties. *N. Fields*

Below: Ex-works 'Super D' 0-8-0 No 49099 passes Chinley North Junction with a freight for the Hope Valley line on 9 April 1959. These engines (their correct classification was 'G1' or 'G2/G2A') were in fact a superheated version of the LNWR 'D' class — hence the name 'Super D'. *N. Fields*

Top: **Without doubt the distinctive landscape of the Peak District forms a fine background in which to photograph almost any sort of train and the area around Chinley was a firm favourite in steam days. Here 'Jubilee' 4-6-0 No 45619** *Nigeria* **is seen at Chinley North Junction with a Manchester to St Pancras express on 19 July 1959.** *N. Fields*

Above: **Heaton Mersey (9F) MPD's Stanier '8F' 2-8-0 No 48115 is setting back into Gowhole Yard on 3 April 1965. Steam working south-east of Manchester to Buxton came to an end from 4 March 1968 with the closure of Northwich (8E), Trafford Park (9E) and Buxton (9L) MPDs, No 48115 being transferred to Rose Grove (10F) MPD.** *N. Fields*

Above: **With a superb display of pyrotechnics Leeds Holbeck (55A) MPD's 'Jubilee' 4-6-0 No 45565 *Victoria* climbs out of Sheffield at Dore & Totley with a Bradford to St Pancras express in May 1959.** *Derek Penney*

Below: **In May 1959 Stanier Class 5 4-6-0 No 44665 moves off Millhouses (41C) MPD as BR Standard Class 4 2-6-0 No 76088 passes with a Sheffield to Manchester via Chinley local.** *Derek Penney*

Top: **In August 1966 'Jubilee' 4-6-0 No 45562 *Alberta* heads a Bradford to Poole working at Millhouses. By this time the last of the 'Jubilees' were attracting a large enthusiast following as the numbers leaning out of the train testify.** *Derek Penney*

Bottom: **An evening picture at Sheffield Midland as 'Peak' No D122 arrives with 1M28, the 3.50pm Bradford to St Pancras on 15 April 1962. It is on these Midland Line duties that the 'Peaks' will be best remembered when speeds up to 100mph were often recorded.** *Cliff Woodhead*

Above: **Permanent way maintenance is in evidence in this picture taken at Shipley Bingley Junction on 20 April 1961 as English Electric Type 4 No D276 passes with an empty carriage stock (ecs) working. All of this class were constructed at Vulcan Foundry excepting D305-D324 which were built by Robert Stephenson & Hawthorns, Darlington.**
Gavin W. Morrison

Below: **No journey over the former Midland main line from St Pancras would be complete without a picture on the Settle & Carlisle. Stanier Class 5 No 45254 is seen crossing Ais Gill Viaduct as it blasts up the last mile to Ais Gill summit in May 1966.** *Derek Penney*

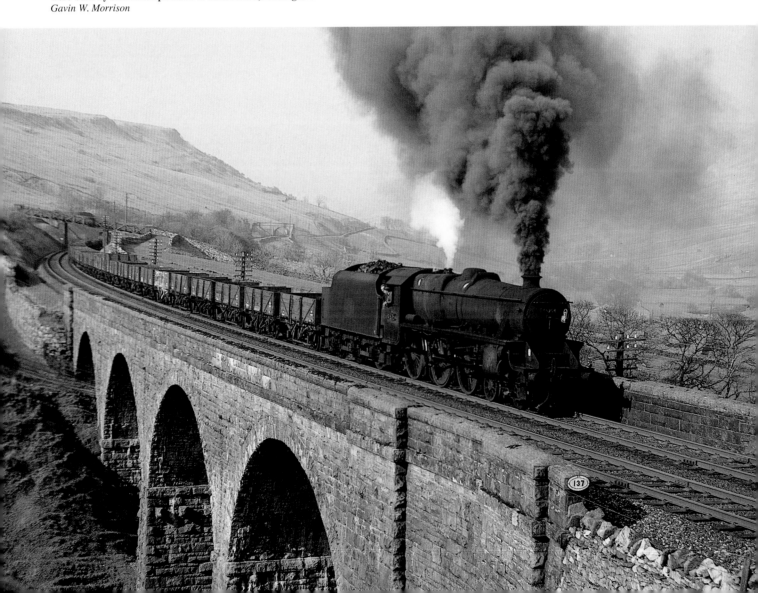

Top: **On the penultimate day of passenger operations, 1 May 1964, Ivatt 2-6-2T No 41225 is at Wellingborough London Road with the 8.10am motor working from Northampton.** *Ken Fairey*

Bottom: **This delightful picture of the well-kept station at Amlwch in November 1963 shows a two-car Derby Lightweight unit awaiting departure for Bangor.** *Historical Model Railway Society/Colour-Rail*

3
Push-Pull to DMU

Long before branch line services were decimated by Beeching in the 1960s railway companies were looking for ways of reducing operating costs. The branch line train which wandered along country byways often produced very little remuneration by comparison to the cost of keeping the large numbers of staff that were needed to run the services. Even in the days before World War 1 companies began to introduce railmotors and push-pull or auto trains often by dispensing with the guard, the driver controlling the train, the fireman staying on the engine. The one significant advantage of the railmotor or push-pull train was that there was no need to run a locomotive round the train at the end of each journey. Some of these early push-pull trains could be very dusty and dirty and some suffered from severe vibration.

Notwithstanding these shortcomings these trains carried out their duties for a number of years, the last surviving railmotors, one of L&YR and one of LNWR origin, both being withdrawn as British Railways property in 1948.

The LMS and British Railways adopted a vacuum-powered control system for their push-pull trains which was very similar to that which had been adopted as standard by the LNER. An auxiliary vacuum-controlled steam regulator valve was fitted and on locomotives with inside cylinders it was located inside the smokebox. This extra steam valve could be seen on the side of the locomotives so equipped and also had an additional flexible vacuum pipe at each end. Classes fitted with this apparatus included the MR Class 2P 0-4-4Ts and Class 3F 0-6-0Ts, the LNWR Class 1P 2-4-2Ts and Class 2F 0-6-2T 'Coal Tanks'. Also fitted were L&YR Class 5 2-4-2Ts (LMS Class 2P), the Fowler Class 3P 2-6-2Ts, Stanier 0-4-4Ts and BR Standard 84xxx 2-6-2Ts. The driving cab ends on the LMS vehicles were very similar in design to several types of LNWR and LMS electric multiple-units, having large sun visors over each window. The LMR push-pull services had ended by the mid-1960s — one late survivor was the operation from Chorley to Horwich principally used by BR staff who were employed at the former L&YR works at Horwich.

The Modernisation Plan of 1955 envisaged the replacement of more than half of Britain's passenger services with diesel multiple-units. The 1955 proposal was for a fleet of some 4,600 vehicles. Following a favourable report made by senior railway officers to the Railway Executive in 1952 who had studied the use of lightweight diesel trains both at home and abroad it was decided initially to replace steam services with diesel railcars in two areas: the West Riding (Leeds, Bradford, Harrogate and Halifax); and West Cumberland (Carlisle, Silloth, Whitehaven, Workington and Penrith). To obtain a satisfactory power-to-weight ratio it was decided to construct the railcars integrally of light alloy. Eight two-car sets were made at Derby for the West Riding scheme and then 13 for the West Cumberland scheme. Body length was 57ft overall. Each two-car set (motor car and driving trailer) seated 114 second-class and 16 first-class passengers.

Steam push-pull services on the Banbury to Buckingham line were selected for an experiment to introduce a diesel replacement in an attempt to prove their viability. Before the service was dieselised the steam push-pull services had been losing £14,000 per annum with receipts of no more than £50 a month. The introduction of railcars boosted receipts to £250 to £300 a month, the exact amount depending on the season. Nevertheless, even the best month's working of the whole three-year experiment still showed an operating deficit of £400 and the annual loss could not be improved beyond a figure of £4,700.

By 1962 the BR fleet of some 4,100 diesel railcars had been brought into being over a period of six years. During this period the transition was performed comparatively painlessly with the planned training of operating and maintenance staff.

Today the first generation of BR DMUs has only recently been made extinct. At the top end of today's range are high-tech tilting Virgin Super Voyager units which have now heralded the virtual end of diesel-hauled timetabled passenger trains in Britain, the exceptions being the overnight sleeper services which are still locomotive hauled.

Below: **The single line from Weedon to Leamington was worked by LNWR engines, the Webb 2-4-2Ts being eventually replaced by Ivatt Class 2 2-6-2Ts as depicted in this picture of an auto train at Southam & Long Itchington in May 1957. Closure to passengers came on 15 September 1958 and after cement trains which ran from Marton Junction to Rugby ceased in March 1985, the line was lifted in 1987.** *John Edgington*

Bottom: **The 3¾-mile branch line from Seaton Junction to Uppingham was one of the best examples of the traditional English branch line. Here BR Standard 2-6-2T No 84008 awaits departure from Seaton Junction with a push-pull working to Uppingham on 10 April 1965. The line was unusual in that to get to Uppingham the train had to cross the rival Midland line twice to climb out of the Welland Valley.** *Bryan Hicks*

Above: **Picturesque Seaton Junction, this picture capturing one auto train as it leaves for the Uppingham branch and the second waiting to depart for Stamford. The line was well known for its use of Johnson 0-4-4Ts and the former London, Tilbury & Southend Railway 4-4-2T No 41975 in the 1950s. The passenger service to Uppingham was withdrawn on 13 June 1960.** *John Carter*

Below: **Derby Lightweight single-car unit No 79901 leaves Verney Junction for Bletchley in this view taken in July 1964. The trackbed of the former Metropolitan Railway line to Quainton Road curves away to the right. Today the stations at Verney Junction, Claydon and Marsh Gibbon & Poundon still retain their platform edges.**
Tommy Tomalin/Colour-Rail

Top: **Chester Cathedral is prominent in the background of this picture as a pair of BR Derby-built two-car units crosses the Dee Bridge with a Manchester to Llandudno local in March 1965. Today, the two lines on the left of this picture have been removed.**
Martin S. Welch

Bottom: **A Derby Lightweight two-car unit stops at Betws-y-Coed with a Blaenau Ffestiniog to Llandudno Junction service in June 1962. This 28-mile branch line is now promoted as the Conwy Valley Line and the large station buildings at Betws-y-Coed still survive as does Pullman car *Emerald*, seen here as a Camping Coach for holidaymakers.**
Cliff Woodhead

Above: **Exactly one week before closure to passenger services BR Standard Class 2 2-6-2T No 84025 propels empty stock from Bolton to Horwich past Horwich Fork Junction on 20 September 1965. No 84025 was withdrawn in December 1965.** *Peter J. Fitton*

Below: **At the end of the 1¾-mile branch from Blackrod was the terminus at Horwich. In this 1964 view BR Standard Class 2 2-6-2T No 84019 awaits departure with an auto train for Blackrod and behind is the through train to Bolton. Services over the branch were mainly for the employees at the former Lancashire & Yorkshire Railway works.** *John Edgington*

Top: **A Derby-built two-car M796xx series DMU forms the first part of this four-car set at it passes Hest Bank as the 10.20 Carlisle to Morecambe Promenade on 12 July 1964. This was a timetabled train on which day return tickets were available. The bars over the windows were due to the restricted clearances on the Maryport & Carlisle line.**
Derrick Codling

Above: **This delightful study depicts three-car Calder Valley (Class 110) DMU awaiting departure under the canopy at Penrith station in September 1961. Amongst the most interesting DMUs on BR, they were powered by four 180hp Rolls-Royce diesel engines.**
George Staddon/Colour-Rail

Above: **On the former GC&NS joint line from Marple to Macclesfield a Metropolitan-Cammell twin unit awaits departure from the platform at High Lane on 12 March 1966.** *N. Fields*

Below: **Two three-car BRCW DMUs form the 1Z16 ADEX (Additional Day Excursion) Buxton to Blackpool North as it passes Kirkham & Wesham on 18 April 1965.** *Derrick Codling*

Top: **The crew pose for the camera in this picture taken in June 1963 as Fowler 2-6-4T No 42378 heads a down local near Morecambe South Junction north of Lancaster.** *Derek Penney*

Botton: **A delightful study of Stanier 2-6-4T No 42610 preparing to leave Mill Hill Broadway with a commuter train in July 1961. One year later No 42610 was reallocated to Rowsley (17C) MPD.** *John Carter*

4
Local Passenger

It was local traffic using the network of lines in the Leeds/Bradford conurbation that was chosen by British Railways for replacement with diesel railcars. These short suburban and inter-urban services of dusty maroon, non-compartment coaches had been hauled by a variety of former LMS, North Eastern Railway and Great Northern Railway tank engines on the intricate network of lines amongst the terraced houses and mills of blackened millstone grit of West Yorkshire.

The first delivery was of eight two-car Derby Lightweight sets. To improve on the steam trains that they were to replace the units had to have a much higher power-to-weight ratio. Each two-car set had four 125hp Leyland diesel engines giving 500hp with a theoretical power-to-weight ratio of 9hp/ton against the feeble 2-3hp/ton exerted by the typical steam trains they replaced.

The success of these early BR builds led to the decision to increase the production rate. A number of independent companies were invited to supply diesel multiple units (DMUs); four of these firms followed the lightweight design. These were Park Royal, Cravens of Sheffield, Gloucester Carriage & Wagon and Wickham of Ware, all using integral body and underframe designs to keep down the weight of the vehicles. Heavier units were built by Metro-Cammell which increased their usage with their ability to haul tail traffic.

Having taken over many commuter and branch line services it was thought that the benefits offered by DMUs with their ability to provide quick turn-round times could be applied to medium and long-distance trains. With these advantages in mind the North Eastern Region saw the concept of an Inter-City DMU as ideal for the replacement of the steam-worked services between Hull and Liverpool Lime Street, a route featuring steep gradients through the Pennines and a number of important intermediate stations.

An order was duly placed for a design known as the 'Inter Cities Diesel Multiple Unit HL' (HL=Hull–Liverpool). These were constructed at Swindon Works and were delivered in 1960. The new sets were initially allocated to Leeds Neville Hill depot, a surprise move as Hull Botanic Gardens had been recently modernised

as a diesel depot. The depot at Neville Hill had one major advantage — an engine drop pit — a facility that was vital to the maintenance of the Inter-City DMUs. The interior layout of these units was a compromise between the earlier suburban DMUs and locomotive-hauled stock. The motor composites were open, similar to many DMUs, but having the added comforts of high-backed seats and curtains to the windows in both first and second-class accommodation.

The Leeds to Manchester journey time was reduced from 78-87min depending on the number of stops, to 68min. As with the earlier DMUs this was due to the higher power-to-weight ratio giving faster acceleration on gradients. These 'Trans-Pennine' units settled down to give a good service for the next 10 years until the opening of the M62, when increased road competition made the rail journey times between Lancashire and Yorkshire look tediously slow.

Having replaced steam traction on the the Liverpool to Hull services over Diggle with the Trans-Pennine DMUs in 1960/61, the progressive North Eastern Region turned its attention to modernising the Calder Valley line, once again with DMUs to meet the conditions faced on that route. An order was placed with the Birmingham Railway Carriage & Wagon Co of Smethwick, in conjunction with the Drewry Car Co for 30 high-powered three-car sets which would replace almost all of the steam-hauled passenger trains on that route.

These were built during 1961 and were supplied in two batches, the first 20 for the North Eastern Region and another 10 for the London Midland Region. Each set was powered by four Rolls-Royce 180hp series 138D engines and comprised a driving motor second, a trailer second and a driving motor composite. The new DMUs entered service on New Year's Day 1962, replacing a somewhat mixed bag of steam workings which ran from a variety of sources, with the Sowerby Bridge-Manchester section forming the central core, the other main line steam service running between Normanton and Manchester. Under the Total Operations Processing System (TOPS) classification the units became Class 110.

Right: **Midland Line commuter working. Here condensing Fowler 2-6-2T No 40038 passes Mill Hill Yard in the summer of 1960. No 40038 remained in traffic at Kentish Town (14B) MPD until August 1961 when it was withdrawn.** *John Carter*

Below: **A final picture of Midland Line commuter working as Fowler 2-6-4T No 42300 passes the signalbox at Welsh Harp Junction. Situated between the north end of Cricklewood and Hendon station, it took its name from a nearby reservoir. It wasn't a junction as such, merely a connection between the fast and slow lines.** *John Carter*

Left: **Kirkby-in-Ashfield is captured in this picture taken on 1 August 1963 as Fairburn 2-6-4T No 42089 arrives with a local train. One of (41) members of the class constructed at Brighton, it was originally based on the Southern Region at Stewarts Lane (73A) MPD and was transferred to Kirkby-in-Ashfield in November 1961. The blue and white liveried bus in the background belonged to the Midland General Bus Company.** *John Carter*

Above: No evidence is visible of the forthcoming electrification in this picture taken at South Kenton as Stanier 2-6-4T No 42573 heads north with an evening commuter working. For many years a Rugby (2A) MPD locomotive, No 42573 was transferred to Willesden in July 1962 from where it worked until withdrawn in January 1964. *John Carter*

Below: The current was switched on between Chalfont and Chesham on 14 August 1960 enforcing the retirement of the oldest passenger coaches in regular BTC use. Here Ivatt 2-6-2T No 41270 awaits departure from Chesham. By June 1961 No 41270 was reallocated to Exmouth Junction (72A) MPD working out its days in the West Country. *John Carter*

Top: **With less than a year to go before withdrawal Bristol Barrow Road (22A) MPD's '2P' 4-4-0 No 40486 is captured near Halesowen Junction as it works the 4.35pm Birmingham New Street to Gloucester in May 1956. These 4-4-0s were a Fowler rebuild with piston valves and superheater of the original Johnson engines built in 1912.** *John Edgington*

Above: **Complete with yellow warning panel, BR/Sulzer Type 2 No D5026 is seen on the slow line in Tring Cutting with an up local on 25 May 1963. The weight of some of the early diesels gave rise to the problem of braking force capability. Some locomotives were paired with a brake tender when used on heavy freight.** *T. B. Owen*

Above: **Allocated to Shrewsbury (89A) MPD in December 1962, BR Standard Class 4 2-6-4T No 80102 is carrying express headlamp lights as it awaits departure from Shrewsbury in June 1963.** *John Edgington*

Below: **Closed to passengers on 5 March 1962, the line from Northampton to Bedford sees Ivatt Class 2 2-6-2T No 41225 passing Ravenstone Wood Junction with a two-coach local.** *John Carter*

Top: **A summer view in the Hope Valley as BR/Sulzer Type 2 No D7598 departs from Edale with a Sheffield to Chinley local on 9 July 1966. The diesels had replaced the Ivatt Class 2 2-6-0s that were used on these workings.** *Bryan Hicks*

Bottom: **'Peak' No D188 is passing Leeds Wortley Junction North with an ecs working on 20 September 1963. The Class 46s as they became known had six Brush traction motors instead of Crompton Parkinson, making them the precursors to Class 47, D188 becoming 46051.** *Gavin W. Morrison*

Right: **Regular performer on the Worth Valley branch from Keighley to Oxenhope, Ivatt Class 2 2-6-2T No 41326 arrives at Haworth on 30 June 1960. In an attempt to improve the service and reduce operating costs DMUs were introduced shortly after this picture was taken but final closure was inevitable when the DMUs were withdrawn from the line. Closure brought to an end 95 years of passenger working on 30 December 1961.** *Gavin W. Morrison*

Above: **On the former Lancashire & Yorkshire Railway line from Liverpool to Preston BR/Sulzer Type 2 No D5061 catches a brief glimpse of sunlight as it passes Midge Hall on 18 May 1968. The whole class was built at three BR workshops: Derby, Crewe and Darlington. Nos D5000-29, 5066-75 and 5114-50 were built at Derby, D5030-65/76-93 at Crewe, and D5094-5113 at Darlington. The first Class 24 withdrawal was in November 1967 when No D5051 was taken out of service apparently after fire damage, although information is scarce.** *T. B. Owen*

Right: **Stanier Class 3 2-6-2T No 40075 has charge of the three-coach 3.35pm local from Normanton to Sowerby Bridge as it passes Heaton Lodge Junction on 25 June 1960. A long-term resident of Normanton (55E) MPD, No 40075 was to continue in traffic for a further year from that depot until July 1961 when it was withdrawn.** *Freddie Bullock*

A superb portrait of a classic locomotive. One of 10 members of this class to remain unnamed throughout their working lives, 'Patriot' class 4-6-0 No 45547 has been coaled and awaits its next turn of duty at Willesden (1A) MPD. Willesden was often host to over 100 engines, some invariably priming the north London air with coal tar. It wasn't difficult to see how 'Willesden Grey Livery' got its name. *John Carter*

5
On Shed and Works

The Modernisation Plan published in 1955 proposed the replacement of steam with diesel and electric motive power and in the years between 1957 and 1968 over 16,000 steam locomotives were removed from service, some almost new.

Keeping steam engines 'on the road' required a small army of workers, the work often being dirty and unpleasant and from the 1940s it was becoming increasingly difficult to recruit staff. The improved working conditions brought about by the introduction of diesels was a very significant reason for replacing steam traction.

In order to keep a steam locomotive running it had to make regular visits to a shed or motive power depot and required constant attention from both shed staff and crew. When coming on shed there were numerous checks to be carried out by driver and fireman, some of them being extremely dirty. For example on a large passenger locomotive there were some 60 points which required oiling before the engine moved off shed and before that it would have required hours of attention from the shed staff. In order to raise steam the fire would have been lit hours earlier.

In terms of efficiency a steam locomotive would spend only approximately a third of its time actually working, the rest of its life being spent on shed. In theory diesels run much longer without attention and should run 23 out of 24 hours, although in practice this is rarely achieved. Lost time is sometimes due to the locomotives having to queue at depots to take their turn for servicing. Nevertheless a diesel engine should be able to perform the work carried out by three steam locomotives.

Having said that, efforts had been made by the LMS to improve the efficiency of shed operations. Camden was one of 13 depots which an LMS Traffic Committee proposal of 24 May 1933 had chosen for improvement. Here locomotive disposal procedures were as follows: 1. Watering 2. Coaling 3. Dropping Fire 4. Turning 5. Inspection, prior to disposal. At the end of 1959 there were 470 steam locomotive depots on BR with the total number of staff needed being around 100,000.

Dieselisation had brought about a complete revolution in working practices on the railway. Gone were the dark, dirty and smoky sheds and in their place were clinically clean stabling points and traction maintenance depots.

The first depot to be completely converted for diesel maintenance was Devons Road in London although its life was to be relatively short-lived closing, from 10 September 1964, its duties being divided between Stratford and Willesden.

Diesel engine drivers enjoy comfortable, warm and clean cabs which are a far cry from their roaring, bucking toeholds on the footplate of a steam locomotive where they were frozen on one side and roasted on the other. When diesel engine drivers come on duty registering in at their depot, they are allowed about 10min 'walking time' to get to their locomotive. This includes checking the depot notice boards for operating instructions such as speed restrictions.

The locomotive being used will have already been fuelled, oiled, watered and any minor repairs carried out by the maintenance staff. However, there are still a number of important checks and inspections to be carried out by the driver before he moves off to pick up his train. Depending on the class of locomotive being used these vary between 20 and 30min. On reaching his cab the driver will stow his personal effects, then he will walk round the engine checking everything outside including connecting pipes and cables. Unlike steam days there is no need to oil the locomotive or for the driver to get dirty.

Although much is now automated there are some areas in which skill in handling locomotives is still necessary. Most notably, drivers have to try to avoid wheelslip. This was specially important with the 'Deltics' and other types too which were prone to this problem.

To the outside observer the diesel locomotive driver may not look such a glamorous figure as the engine driver of an old steam engine, but this does not mean that his job is any less fascinating.

Above: **Stanier Pacific No 46240 *City of Coventry* stands over the ash pit at Camden (1B) MPD in July 1963. Camden was fortunate in having a modern ash plant on which the mountains of hot ash could be expeditiously removed in one of the the plant's narrow gauge trucks, an example of which can be seen adjacent to the locomotive's firebox. When withdrawn in October 1964 No 46240 had completed one of the highest mileages of all of the Stanier Pacifics — 1,685,000.** *Paul Riley*

Left: **English Electric 2,700hp Co-Co No DP2 is receiving attention at Camden shed in April 1963. It is carrying the earlier plain green livery with yellow ends. An updated version of No DP2 formed the basis for 50 of the 'D400' class, later Class 50, with flat-fronted cabs requested by BR. After covering over 100,000 miles in traffic without incident No DP2 was considered by many to be the most successful diesel-electric to operate in Britain.** *Geoff Rixon*

Above: **Another portrait of No 46240 *City of Coventry*. After Camden (1B) MPD closed to steam from 9 September 1963, *City of Coventry* was reallocated to Willesden (1A) MPD where it is seen on the occasion of an Railway Correspondence & Travel Society visit on 8 March 1964.**
Martin S. Welch

Below: **In this picture taken on 4 August 1962 'Coronation' class Pacific No 46238 *City of Carlisle* is being turned on Camden's 70ft vacuum-operated turntable before being switched into the appropriate shed road.** *Geoff Rixon*

Top: **The new Cowans Sheldon breakdown crane is seen at Wellingborough on 29 April 1962. The photographer had been asked to record this event by Assistant District Motive Power Superintendent — Wellingborough, Jeff Dentith, but had agreed only if the jib could be lifted.** *Ken Fairey*

Above: **Johnson Midland Class 2F 0-6-0 No 58148 has been in Wellingborough (15A) MPD's No 2 shed for valve and piston repairs and is seen on 28 May 1962. The smokebox repair had been completed for an RCTS trip on the West Bridgford branch on 12 May 1962.** *Ken Fairey*

Top: **The final development of the BR/Sulzer Bo-Bo had a complete redesign of the bodywork. The gangway doors were omitted and the air intake grills were sited in the roof, the whole appearance being enhanced by two-tone green livery. Here newly constructed No D5282 stands outside Derby MPD on 28 June 1964.** *T. B. Owen*

Above: **Introduced five years after the standard BR version, one can only speculate what reasons were behind the construction of the 10 members of the Hudswell Clarke 204hp 0-6-0 Diesel Mechanical shunters. Here No D2513 is pictured outside Derby MPD on 23 March 1967. Two members of this class survive in preservation.** *Ken Fairey*

Left: **Newly constructed BR/Sulzer Bo-Bo Type 2 No D5020 is portrayed outside the test house at Derby Works in October 1959. The first member of the class, No D5000, had commenced revenue-earning service one year earlier on 15 September 1958 when it worked the 9.38am from Derby to Manchester, 12.30pm Manchester to Liverpool Central, returning on the 2.30pm from Liverpool Central to Derby.** *Ray Reed*

Left: **Still in grey primer, Brush-Sulzer Co-Co Type 4 No D1580 undergoes electrical testing at Crewe Works on 26 April 1964. By January 1965, several of this class were transferred from their duties on the GN to the GE where they replaced the English Electric Type 4s, taking over the Liverpool Street to Norwich workings.** *T. B. Owen*

Below: **Crewe North (5A) MPD's 'Patriot' 4-6-0 No 45544 is seen after repair outside the Paint Shop at Crewe Works on 26 June 1960. No 45544 became one of the early casualties of the class when it was withdrawn from Warrington (8B) MPD in November 1961.** *Ray Reed*

Above: **Cleaned by the photographer, Lostock Hall (10D) MPD's Stanier Class 5 No 45000 is seen at Blackpool North (24E) MPD on 21 August 1967. It was rostered to work 1L05, the Mondays/Fridays Only (MFO) 09.35 Blackpool North to Windermere, at that time the only booked steam passenger working north of Preston.** *Peter J. Fitton*

Below: **A rare picture of English Electric Type 4s Nos D378/D255 on Carlisle Upperby (12B) MPD on Sunday 1 September 1963. Carrying the northbound headcode 1S57, it was very unusual to see the tartan style 'Royal Scot' headboard on a diesel locomotive.** *Martin S. Welch*

One of Bushbury (3B) MPD's stud of 'Jubilee' 4-6-0s No 45647 *Sturdee* takes the 'Midlander' out of Birmingham New Street in September 1956. The last members of the class survived until late 1967 when they became the last purely LMS design express passenger locomotives to remain in service. *John Edgington*

6
Express Passenger

During the early 1960s, as passenger train speeds progressively increased, the productivity of BR's locomotive-hauled train sets steadily improved. To facilitate the programming of the LMR 'Under the Wire' services the complete standardisation of all sets working between Euston, Birmingham, Manchester and Liverpool was necessary so that the sets could be interchanged between Manchester or Liverpool. Thus, up trains from Manchester often returned to Liverpool or vice versa. Other advantages of standard formations were seat reservations, restaurant car services and van loading arrangements.

The composition of the Liverpool, Birmingham and Manchester trains reflected their popularity with businessmen. The 11-coach and 12-coach formations included four full-length first-class coaches with about 150 seats; and it became apparent that this fast inter-city travel had attracted a considerable number of passengers away from the London-Manchester and London-Liverpool airline services. Second-class passengers travelled exclusively in centre-corridor stock, which like the first-class accommodation was built specially for the new electric services.

For the first time in British railway history a number of runs appeared in the LMR timetable requiring start-to-stop average times of over 80mph with intermediate pass-to-pass timings of more than 90mph. One innovative piece of timetabling was the use made of the fast Euston to Birmingham trains to introduce a systematically timed service from Birmingham to Liverpool and Manchester. Leaving Euston at 15min past each hour, these trains continued from Birmingham at 5min before each hour to the two Lancashire cities alternately by the direct route. Most morning and evening trains called at Watford Junction in the up direction for the benefit of passengers from the north-western suburbs of London. Similarly calls were made on the down trains to Manchester at Wilmslow and Liverpool trains at Runcorn.

All the expresses from London to North Wales, Blackpool, Carlisle and Scotland went forward from Crewe with diesel traction and also derived substantial accelerations from the electric haulage from Euston to Crewe.

The London Midland electrification was brought into use in three stages, first from Liverpool and Manchester to Crewe, then in sequence to Stafford, Nuneaton and Rugby, and finally through to Euston by April 1966. Electrification of the two loops, from Rugby through Birmingham to Stafford, and from Colwich and Norton Bridge through Stoke-on-Trent to Cheadle Hulme was completed in the summer of 1967.

Highlights of the timetable introduced in May 1970 were the acceleration of seven Anglo-Scottish daytime expresses and the associated recasting of the Euston-North West services. The 1970 accelerations were planned with the knowledge that approval of the Weaver Junction to Glasgow electrification would make a subsequent slowdown for the pre-electrification engineering work necessary.

The new point-to-point times for pairs of Class 50s enabled almost an hour to be cut from the previous schedules between Crewe and Glasgow. The first full year of Anglo-Scottish improvements was very encouraging with passenger journeys increasing by around 30 per cent showing that public response to Inter-City depended very much on a high-speed service.

Another feature of the 1970 timetable was the increase in utilisation of the sets of coaching stock made possible by the accelerations. On the Anglo-Scottish services nine sets of stock — a reduction of four sets — were required to cover 14 Anglo-Scottish trips per day.

The signalling for this 100mph main line was of major importance. The principle employed in the design of the signalling system was that of comprehensive locking panels at the main traffic centres. with subsidiary interlockings at minor junctions controlled electronically from the main centres. The entire signalling for the first 100 miles out of Euston operated from only six control rooms — Euston, Willesden, Watford, Bletchley, Rugby and Nuneaton, the Birmingham loop being controlled by a complex interlocking at New Street with a satellite interlocking at Coventry and a second at Wolverhampton.

Above: Stanier Class 5 4-6-0 No 45110 stands at the buffer stops at Manchester Central in August 1968. A notable monument to Victorian railway architecture, Manchester Central station saw its last train on 3 May 1969, its remaining services being transferred to Piccadilly and Oxford Road. Today the station survives as the GMEX Exhibition Centre. *Derek Penney*

Below: Nottingham (16A) MPD's BR Standard Class 4 4-6-0 No 75063 is seen crossing Marple Wharf Viaduct on 26 May 1958. After short stays at Derby (17A) and (2B) Nuneaton MPDs No 75063 was to see out its days at Shrewsbury (6D) shed from where it was withdrawn in June 1966. *N. Fields*

Left: Crossing the River Dee near Chester racecourse. This time Liverpool Edge Hill (8A) MPD's Stanier Class 5 No 45307 heads an express for the North Wales coast. *John Carter*

Left: An eastbound Trans-Pennine express is in the hands of English Electric Type 4 No D270 as it passes Diggle on 26 October 1965. Although introduced for the LMR's express passenger workings, the class had been supplanted by the Class 50s on certain workings north of Crewe. *N. Fields*

Below: Another Trans-Pennine express, this time hauled by 'Jubilee' 4-6-0 No 45739 *Ulster* as it crosses Longwood Viaduct near Huddersfield on the climb to Standedge summit. *John Carter*

Right: **Long-term resident of Carlisle Kingmoor (12A) MPD, Stanier Class 5 No 45013 is seen arriving at Llandudno Junction in June 1962. On this day Stanier Pacific No 46200** *The Princess Royal* **had also made an appearance at Llandudno Junction with a railtour.** *Derek Penney*

Below: **With the unmistakable profile of Heptonstall Church on the skyline Mirfield (56D) MPD's Stanier Class 5 No 44694 passes Hebden Bridge in August 1966. Earlier that year on 2 May goods facilities at Hebden were withdrawn, the goods yard eventually becoming the station car park.** *Derek Penney*

Left: **English Electric Type 4 No D348 (later No 40148) is arriving at Bradford Exchange with a six-coach Saturdays Only (SO) Weymouth to Bradford train on 1 July 1972. With the spread of the motor car, the increasing truncation of the BR system and the advent of cheap air travel, summer workings to coastal resorts have all but disappeared.** *Peter J. Fitton*

Above: **On 4 April 1970 BR/Sulzer Type 2 No D5266 arrives at Ansdell & Fairhaven with the 09.05 Euston to Blackpool South which it had hauled from Preston. The line was formerly L&Y/LNWR joint but the station is very much in the characteristic L&Y island platform style. The line is still in use but the station buildings were demolished in the early 1970s.** *Peter J. Fitton*

Below: **Introduced in 1967 the English Electric 2,700hp Type 4s were the last express passenger diesel locomotives to be built in this country. Here No D447 is passing the signalbox at St Annes on 19 April 1970 with 1A30, the 08.10 Blackpool South to London Euston which it would haul as far as Crewe where electric traction would take over.** *Peter J. Fitton*

Above: **This superb action shot taken on the West Coast main line near Morecambe South Junction depicts Lower Darwen (24D) MPD's Stanier 2-6-4T No 42483 piloting Stanier Class 5 4-6-0 No 44904 with an up express in July 1962.** *Derek Penney*

Left: **Shortly after leaving Kirkham an unidentified Class 50 heads for Preston with the 09.20 Blackpool North to Euston past Treales signal box on 28 March 1975. The electrification of the WCML was completed in 1974 and over the next two years the need for Class 50s was completely eliminated, the class being transferred to the Western Region. Direct passenger services to Euston from Blackpool were reintroduced in the late 1990s only to be withdrawn again in 2003.** *Peter J. Fitton*

Right: **Stanier Class 5 No 44758 passes Lancaster Ladies Walk with the 17.51 Skipton to Morecambe Promenade on 24 June 1964. A recent visit to Cowlairs Works is given away by the name of the depot being painted on the front buffer beam, an LNER tradition. In this case the allocation is Lancaster Green Ayre (10J) MPD.**
Derrick Codling

Above: **BR/Sulzer Type 2 No D5235 runs alongside the River Lune near Lancaster Green Ayre with the 8.30am Bradford Forster Square to Morecambe Promenade on 4 April 1964.** *Derrick Codling*

Right: **At Lakeside station, near the southern tip of Windermere on 1 July 1956, the crew of 'Patriot' No 45543 *Home Guard* take it easy as they wait for a clear road down the branch to Plumpton Junction, where they will join the Cumberland coast line near Ulverston with their return excursion to Birmingham and Coventry. Of the 34 'Patriots' remaining in the unrebuilt condition, No 45502 *Royal Naval Division* was the first to be withdrawn in September 1960, *Home Guard* being one of the final two locomotives to remain in traffic until November 1962.** *John Edgington*

Top: **In this view, blue-liveried No E26022 is on freight duty at Broadbottom station on 28 May 1969. Note the use of the older BR emblem with the new blue livery — a not uncommon variation at that time.** *N. Fields*

Bottom: **At the former L&Y station at Liverpool Exchange on Sunday 12 April 1959 an LMR Wirral & Mersey EMU set is parked up as Fairburn 2-6-4T No 42063 waits for duty as station pilot.** *Martin S. Welch*

7
Electrification Progress

Britain was at the forefront of experiments with single-phase alternating current (ac) electrification in the early part of the 20th century. However, the benefits of this system were not to be fully exploited until the late 1950s.

In the late Edwardian era two British companies carried out experiments, the LBSCR on its South London line and the Midland Railway between Lancaster and Heysham. There is little doubt that both companies had in mind the electrification of their main lines; the Midland had plans for the conversion of the St Pancras to Bedford line to the low-voltage dc third-rail system as far back as 1900.

The electric traction developments which took place in Lancashire could be described as the epitome of those over the whole country including almost all systems: 1,200V dc, 6.6kV ac at 25 cycles, 3,600V dc overhead, 1,500V dc overhead and finally 25kV ac overhead. The L&Y Liverpool to Southport line originally ran from Liverpool Exchange station to Southport with extensions to Aintree, Ormskirk and over the Liverpool Overhead Railway to Dingle in south Liverpool.

The 6.6kV ac overhead system at 25 cycles was, of course, the Lancaster, Morecambe and Heysham line of the Midland Railway which was opened in 1908.

The next important traction project in Lancashire was the electrification in 1916 of the Manchester to Bury line of the L&Y. However, before this was undertaken mention must be made of the trial of dc overhead equipment at 3,600V on the Bury-Holcombe Brook section.

The conditions under which electric traction developed after 1930 were greatly affected by the coming of the National Electricity Grid and the introduction of the mercury arc rectifier in place of the rotary converter which made it possible to use remote controlled unattended substations.

The first application of the 1,500V dc overhead line system was on the Manchester South Junction & Altrincham Railway under the auspices of the LNER and its Chief Electrical Engineer, H. W. H. Richards, the line being completed in 1931. Thus for the first piece of heavy trunk line electrification to be undertaken in Britain the 1,500V dc overhead system was envisaged.

The system was adopted by the LNER for the Manchester-Sheffield-Wath scheme on which construction was started in 1938, the contractors being British Insulated Cables Limited. Work was suspended during the hostilities, but when the contract was resumed it was found necessary to curtail the original scheme on economic grounds and the original Woodhead tunnels had deteriorated to such an extent it was decided to drive a double track on a new alignment between Woodhead and Dunford Bridge.

The electrification was completed in 1954, and comprised 71 route, and 272 single-track miles, its operation being divided between the London Midland Region, which operated the Manchester to Dunford Bridge section, and the Eastern Region, which worked the remainder to Sheffield and Wath. In postwar years the idea of an all-electric passenger service down the entire Great Central route to Marylebone was frequently discussed. With the difficult coal situation in postwar years it would have been a logical move and would have pre-empted the electrification of the West Coast main line by a good 20 years.

Ten years after opening, the security of the Woodhead route was in doubt in that BR had four trans-Pennine routes and could easily manage with just two. With three of these routes carrying substantial local traffic it was Woodhead that had to close.

The main factors that influenced this decision were the lack of traffic and the savings that could be made upon closure, allegedly amounting to some £65 million before the end of the century. The situation was not helped by the decline in output from Yorkshire collieries which supplied power stations in the west, and the spread of pylons which distributed power over the Pennines.

In any case the Class 76s which operated the line were almost life-expired and almost certainly under-powered for working the 30 wagons making up a modern coal train. With the withdrawal of freight subsidies in 1977 the full costs of track, maintenance and signalling were charged to BR's freight business and the line was closed completely in July 1981, the suburban line from Manchester to Hadfield and Glossop being converted to 25kV operation.

Top: **The Class 501 London District three-car EMUs formed the basis of the Watford and North London 630V dc third-rail services for nearly 30 years. Here a green liveried set is seen arriving at Euston in 1965. These units remained operational until the rapid influx of new Class 313 units saw their complete demise in 1985.** *John Edgington*

Above: **This Class 501 unit waits for departure from Croxley Green with a branch line service to Watford. The electrification of the Euston to Watford line commenced on 15 April 1917, the branch to Croxley Green being energised on 30 October 1922.** *John Edgington*

Above: **This 7 March 1969 picture shows Class AL5 electric No E3059 leaving Rugby with an up express. Introduced in 1961, this class of 40 locomotives was designed and constructed at BR's Doncaster Works.** *Bryan Hicks*

Below: **As part of Coventry's Rail Week on 1 March 1966 blue-liveried Class AL6 No E3200 is on display with an exhibition train in Platform 1. Under TOPS the 100 'AL6' locomotives became Class 86.** *Ray Reed*

Above: **One of the eight three-car sets (later Class 506) that operated the Manchester Piccadilly to Hadfield and Glossop services arrives at Broadbottom on 28 May 1969. The design of these units was based on the ER's (Class 306) units with detail differences. Maintained at Reddish depot, all were withdrawn on 7 December 1984.** *N. Fields*

Below: **After three earlier proposals, electric services on the Manchester South Junction & Altrincham Railway began on 11 May 1931. A service for Altrincham is seen at Manchester Oxford Road on 18 December 1970. The 28.9-mile route was 1,500V dc overhead and was recommended as a national standard by the Weir Report of 1930.** *Peter J. Fitton*

Left: With the exception of the first Class EM1 Bo-Bo electric locomotives built by Metropolitan-Vickers in 1940, all 57 of the Woodhead electric freight locomotives were built at Gorton Works between 1950 and 1953. Here No 26035 is seen outside the works on 26 June 1960. Designed by Sir Nigel Gresley for the Manchester, Sheffield and Wath electrification scheme, 32 of the fleet were still operational when the line closed to freight traffic on 18 July 1981. *Ray Reed*

Left: This 3 June 1966 picture sees green-liveried Class EM1 No 26045 at the head of a typical train, consisting of mostly 16-ton BR mineral wagons on the climb to Woodhead at Crowden. The inauguration of electric traction between Sheffield and Manchester took place on 14 September 1954 when 'EM2' No 27000 was ceremonially whistled away from Sheffield Victoria by Sir Brian Robertson, chairman of the British Transport Commission. *N. Fields*

Below: Class EM1s Nos 26010 and 26011 head an eastbound freight into Woodhead Tunnel on 19 July 1972. When the double-track Woodhead New Tunnel was opened to traffic in June 1954, the two single-line tunnels became redundant. Twelve years later in 1966 the up line tunnel was opened for contractors preparing it for the laying of a power line which can be clearly seen in this picture. *Peter J. Fitton*

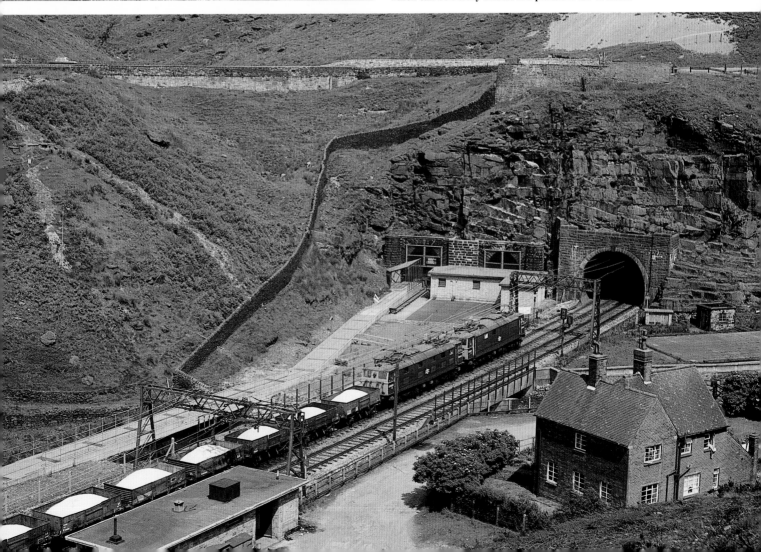

Right: **A Manchester to Bury Class 504 EMU passes the motive power depot at Bury (26D) in October 1964. The first section of electric railway in the Manchester area opened on 29 July 1913 when services began on the L&Y line from Bury to Holcombe Brook.** *P. W. Robinson*

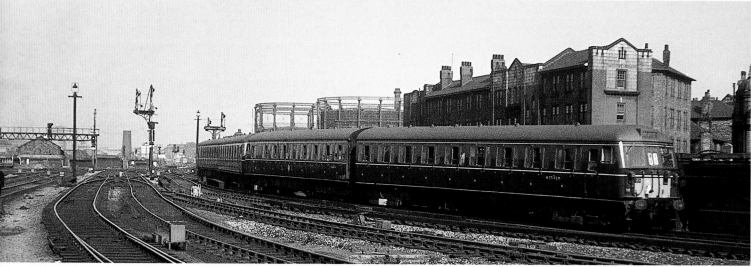

Above: **This picture taken on 26 August 1964 depicts an EMU set leaving Manchester Victoria for Bury. It is interesting to note that the unit carries an oil tail lamp which was the normal practice. Between Manchester Victoria and Bury there were six stations, but two new ones were built in the 1930s to cater for new suburbs at Besses o' th' Barn in 1933, then Bowker Vale in 1938.** *Derrick Codling*

Left: **The L&Y's Liverpool to Southport electrification was inaugurated in 1904, additional extensions to Aintree and Ormskirk opening in 1906 and 1913 respectively. Here a Wirral & Mersey set is passing Bank Hall (27A) MPD in 1960. The leading vehicle, No M28348M, is a motor brake second, part of a large order for new open stock introduced by the LMS in 1939.** *J. Agnew Collection*

Above: **EMU No M29022M leaves Platform 5 at Lancaster Castle as the 13.45 to Morecambe (Promenade) on 26 August 1964. This platform was re-electrified in 1974 as part of the standard 25kV system. High-voltage electrification was pioneered on this line in 1908.** *Derrick Codling*

Below: **1 January 1966 was the last day of operation of electric services on the Lancaster, Morecambe & Heysham line, the final train being the 23.10 Morecambe (Promenade) to Lancaster Castle. Here unit No M29021M approaches Lancaster Green Ayre on 29 August 1964.** *Gavin W. Morrison*

Top: **Clean Stanier Class 5 No 44872 marshalls a parcels coach at Crewe station on 15 August 1958. The station is undergoing roof repairs and the station canopies which were replaced during modernisation for electrification are also visible.** *Martin S. Welch*

Bottom: **The pride of Canklow (41D) MPD, Johnson Class 1F 0-6-0 No 41835, is captured on station pilot duties at Rotherham Masboro in 1958. No 41835 was the only 1960s survivor of this class not to have been rebuilt with a Belpaire firebox, and retained the Salter type safety valves.** *Derek Penney*

8
Shunting Duties

As far back as 1927 the management of the London Midland & Scottish Railway, under the direction of Lord Stamp, embarked upon an investigation to review the costs of marshalling and sorting wagons. The size of the problem could be judged from the fact that more than half of the freight-engine hours was taken up by shunting locomotives.

It became obvious that it was essential that some economy be effected to reduce shunting costs and from this Sir Ernest Lemon, the LMS Vice-President, set about a scheme to thoroughly investigate the modernisation of marshalling yards and the methods of shunting them.

An in-depth study was made into the locomotives employed in shunting work and the costs of these units in traffic. At that time shunting duties were mainly in the hands of the standard '3F' 0-6-0Ts and a variety of locomotives with pre-Grouping origins. The study covered all possible types of shunting unit, diesel locomotives with both mechanical and electrical transmissions, petrol locomotives with rubber tyres for operation on both rail and road as well as Sentinel high-pressure geared locomotives.

At that time most British railway companies had operated, in their civil engineers departments, both narrow and standard gauge petrol shunters but it was the diesel locomotive which appeared to be the most promising traction unit for shunting. Before delivery of any trial batch constructed by private builders the LMS had produced its own standard-gauge diesel locomotive. This experimental unit was built on the frames of an old Johnson Midland Class 1F 0-6-0T at Derby Works and emerged in late 1932. This unit, numbered 1831, was put into traffic in 1934 and despite various problems it did prove the effectiveness of the diesel shunter and set the pattern for the programme of experimental work carried out by the LMS up to 1939.

Contracts for nine new diesel shunting locomotives had been placed in 1932 with five different makers; eight were to have mechanical transmission and one electrical, with delivery being in the period up to 1934, some not actually being put into running stock until 1935. The first of these was built by the Hunslet Engine

Co in Leeds and was a private venture appearing at the British Industries Fair in Birmingham in February 1932. The second locomotive was also from this builder, initially numbered 7401 but soon renumbered 7051, and was put into service in January 1934. After loan to the War Department it was sold to the Admiralty in 1943. The next locomotive to appear was built by the recently opened diesel locomotive department of Sir W. G. Armstrong-Whitworth of Scotswood-on-Tyne in 1933. Eventually renumbered 7408, it was allocated the BR number 13000 which it never carried, being taken out of service for scrapping in December 1949.

The next locomotive to be constructed was of particular interest, being the only one by that maker ever to work on an English railway. Built by Harland & Wolff Ltd in Belfast, it was numbered 7057 by the LMS. This locomotive was passed to the Northern Counties Committee (NCC) who gave it the number 22 and was passed to the Ulster Transport Authority (UTA), which took it out of service in 1965.

The results of the LMS trials with the nine prototypes proved that for intensive yard shunting work, an installed engine of about 300-350bhp was needed. It was thus the 350bhp 0-6-0 diesel-electric became the basic LMS diesel locomotive. The newly formed British Railways started investing heavily in 350bhp, diesel-electric shunters which were based on the later LMS design and went on to construct no fewer than 1,193 virtually identical units between 1952 and 1962. No further design was ever produced and although shunting is today a small fraction of what it once was, the 350bhp units as Class 08 and 09 remain in use across the system more than 50 years later.

Numerous other lower-powered or lighter designs were produced by a variety of manufacturers in both 0-4-0 and 0-6-0 configurations, many having already been produced in large quantities for industrial service but surprisingly neither the Class 03/04 or 08/09 design was ever built new for industry. As BR steadily withdrew them from service they became very popular as secondhand units, with a number finding use on preserved railways.

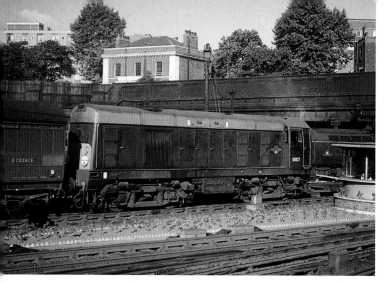

Left: This picture taken at Euston in 1961 sees English Electric Type 1 Bo-Bo No D8037 on station pilot duties. Not all BR Type 1s were built to the same design, Nos D8000-D8127 being fitted with disc train reporting equipment, whilst Nos D8128-D8327 were fitted with four-character route indicators. Some of the class were not constructed at Vulcan Foundry, Nos D8050-D8127 being built by RSH Ltd. *Cliff Woodhead*

Left: Former Midland Railway Class 0F 0-4-0ST No 41537 is seen at Gloucester Tramway Crossing on 20 October 1962. This class of eight dock tanks were the only pure Midland locomotives to be built with outside cylinders and outside Walschaerts valve gear, the others being the Somerset & Dorset 2-8-0s which were of joint stock. *N. Simms*

Below: Classified 08 by BR, this type derived from an English Electric prototype of 1934 and totalled almost 1,200 units. Here No D3767 is seen carrying its original dark green livery with no yellow panels at Birmingham Central Goods Depot during a freight handling demonstration in June 1959. *John Edgington*

Top: **Class 0F 0-4-0ST No 47009, one of five built at Horwich after Nationalisation, in 1953, with larger side tanks and coal space, has received the attention of a graffiti artist in this picture taken at Birkenhead (6C) MPD on 24 May 1959.** *Ray Reed*

Above: **Still in remarkably good condition after 40-plus years in service, Midland 0-4-0ST No 41533 is captured at the Staveley Ironworks complex on 21 December 1963. No 41533, part of the original Deeley '1528' class, was the first of the 1921 series.** *Derek Penney*

Above: **Condensing 'Jinty' 3F 0-6-0T No 47211 pilots '0F' 0-4-0ST No 47008 back to Lostock Hall MPD on 11 March 1964. No 47008 had spent the morning shunting Greenbank Sidings but had to be piloted because it was too short to operate the track circuiting.** *Peter J. Fitton*

Below: **One of some 230 Barton Wright-designed tender engines rebuilt as saddle tanks to replace older types, No 11324 is seen at Horwich Works on 16 September 1962. As a departmental locomotive it retained its LMS number until withdrawn.** *Peter J. Fitton*

Above: **Late afternoon light highlights the clean lines of Ivatt Class 2 2-6-2T No 41222 as it goes about its duties as Carlisle station south end pilot on 11 February 1965.** *John Edgington*

Below: **BR 0-6-0 shunter No D3173 is seen near Carlisle Kingmoor with a Travelling Post Office (TPO) on 23 July 1972. With East Coast main line diversions through Carlisle that day the next down train was the 'Flying Scotsman' with No D9020.** *Peter J. Fitton*

Top: **'Jinty' 0-6-0 No 47435 passes over Metropolitan Widened Lines to the Southern Region at Stamford Brook station with coal empties from the Midland's depot at West Kensington *en route* to Cricklewood.** *John Carter*

Bottom: **In the snow-covered landscape of the Pennines Brush-Sulzer Type 4 No D1545 climbs the 1 in 100 past Horton in Ribblesdale with a lightweight freight on 29 November 1969.** *Gavin W. Morrison*

9
Freight Operations

The Reshaping of British Railways, better known as the Beeching Report, published in 1963, considered freight traffic to be all-important to the future of the railways as a nationwide system. Its recommendations for freight services were much less publicised than the headlines of branch line and station closures. The forward-looking approach of the report to freight traffic was largely overlooked. In 1961 the British Railways Board had commissioned a study of contemporary freight handling. This study had dealt with railfreight and 'traffic not on rail' and analysed the movement of 223 million tons of non-railborne traffic in 1960, its aim being not to close lines and goods depots but to target potential growth.

The railway infrastructure in 1961 had changed little since Victorian times, the average turn-round for a British Railways wagon being 11.9 working days, loaded transit times averaging two days. This allowed each wagon no more than 25 loaded journeys a year, each averaging 67 miles. The size of the problem was enormous.

In his report Beeching had classified freight traffic into three categories: coal, minerals and general merchandise. Coal encompassed all coal products and in 1961 was marginally profitable. Mineral traffic encompassed minerals like iron ore, limestone and china clay and included semi-finished steel, bricks, tar, fertiliser and even sugar beet. In the main, general merchandise dealt with wagonload freight, the bulk of which was manufactured goods. This group also included oil and petrol which was an indication of the lesser importance of this traffic in 1961, the last two groups being heavy loss makers. The profitability of each traffic was analysed by its costs, these comprising road collection and delivery, terminal expenses, trip working, marshalling, trunk haulage, provision of wagons and documentation.

By restructuring the freight network around approximately 100 depots and investing in freightliner services most of the general freight traffic could be retained. The Report's proposals were an ambitious Freightliner network and the centralisation of less-than-wagonload freight at about 100 new depots. Looking back today we can see that many of the Beeching recommendations were correct as the costs of road collection, terminals, trip working and marshalling have been abolished by concentrating most freight traffic in block loads travelling between private sidings.

The one area of serious miscalculation that the plan proposed was that customers would continue to rely on rail transport for their goods, even if this meant that there would be the additional cost of the time taken for the double handling with loading and unloading. In later years BR's Railfreight sector made no pretence about its lack of interest in this business.

The new concept of liner trains was to have been the main method of winning less-than-trainload traffic back to the railways. With a striking similarity to the modern Speedlink map, the Beeching proposals featured more than 50 depots which would handle 29 million tons of traffic each year, increasing to 39 million tons by 1973. The cost of this exercise was estimated to be £100 million, depots costing £16 million, locomotives and wagons £34 million, road vehicles £25 million, as well as £25 million for containers.

Beeching's positive attitude towards railfreight is in stark contrast to the feelings aroused in most of us when the name Beeching is mentioned. In his Report it is clear that he thought that by investing in new technology he intended to build an intensively used, nationwide Freightliner network which would operate alongside a profitable bulk freight railway.

In conclusion not all of the recommendations made by Beeching have been vindicated, but his proposals for freight were forward-thinking and positive. The most successful of today's freight operation, the merry-go-round coal train, was included in his plan which recommended increased braking of wagons with improved design for higher capacity. The blueprint for a successful bulk freight operation was laid out together with plans for a nationwide Freightliner network.

His plans for the devastation of rural passenger services may now be seen as misguided but his proposals for railborne freight were remarkably astute and have stood the test of time.

Right: **Derby-built BR/Sulzer Bo-Bo Type 2 No D5068 approaches Harrow with a down fitted goods in July 1962. At this time Willesden-based Class 24s (as they became under TOPS) had taken over local and ecs workings out of Euston.**
Cliff Woodhead

Above: **This picture taken north of Hatch End in May 1963 depicts an unidentified Stanier Class 8F 2-8-0 heading coal empties from Stonebridge Park power station to Shipley Colliery in the Erewash Valley. The very distinctive 40-ton side discharge coal hopper wagons were part of a batch of 30 received by the LMS in 1929. The power station at Stonebridge Park provided electricity for the dc lines out of Euston and Broad Street until it closed in 1966.** *John Carter*

Left: **During its one-year allocation to Wellingborough (15A) MPD Ivatt Class 4 2-6-0 No 43019 heads an up pick-up goods near Finedon on 8 March 1963. No 43019 became one of only six members of the class to survive into the final year of steam in 1968.** *Ken Fairey*

Above: **A timeless study on the Leicester West Bridge branch as Johnson Midland 0-6-0 No 58148 heads the branch goods. Nos 58143, 58148 and 58182 were concentrated at Coalville (15D) MPD from which depot they operated until December 1963.** *John Carter*

Below: **The former Midland Railway station at Spondon is the setting for this picture of two Stanier '8Fs' as they speed through light engine on 5 March 1963. The leading locomotive, No 48193, has COLK marked on its smokebox door, presumably working from Colwick MPD.** *John Edgington*

Above: **Paired with a Fowler tender, Stanier '8F' No 48555 heads a train of empty ICI hoppers from Winnington (Cheshire Lines Committee) to Peak Forest near Chinley on 19 July 1959. This Northwich (8E)-based 2-8-0 was constructed by the LNER during World War 2.** *N. Fields*

Left: **This 1966 picture depicts former Crosti-boilered '9F' 2-10-0 No 92021 hard at work climbing the 1 in 105 gradient towards Standedge summit near Linthwaite. Built in 1955 Nos 92020-92029 were fitted with Crosti boilers which had a second drum under the boiler to preheat the feed water. The hot gases which were ejected at a chimney on the right-hand side in front of the firebox passed through both, the design encountering serious corrosion problems and complaints from enginemen.** *Freddie Bullock*

Top: **Stanier '8F' 2-8-0 No 48208 passes the former Cheshire Lines Committee box at Cheadle West on 6 August 1965. Until October 1965 there were eight Cheadle signalboxes. Cheadle West box controlled the exit at the western end of Cheadle Sidings. Cheadle Hulme, Cheadle Village Junction and Cheadle Goods were ex-London & North Western Railway. Cheadle Heath North and Cheadle Heath South were both former Midland Railway. In addition to Cheadle West, the boxes at Cheadle Junction and Cheadle Station were ex-CLC.** *N. Fields*

Above: **A two-tone green liveried Brush-Sulzer Type 4 passes through the station at Grindleford with a short freight on 6 April 1972. Designated Class 47 under TOPS, the class had a 20-ton axle loading which gave it a wide route availability.** *Martin S. Welch*

Right: **With Stanier '8F' No 48327 leading and No 48529 assisting at the rear the pair power a rake of empty coal wagons up the 1 in 30 gradient to Chequerbent on the Kenyon Junction to Bolton line on 31 May 1968. One of the earliest railways to be opened, the Bolton & Leigh Railway was engineered by George Stephenson and opened on 1 August 1828, preceding the Liverpool & Manchester Railway by more than two years.** *N. Fields*

Top: **With the ex-LNWR semaphores featuring strongly in this picture, Stanier Class 5 4-6-0 No 45448 passes Crows Nest Junction near Hindley in Lancashire on 21 July 1968. The lines to the left go to Blackrod and those to the right to Manchester via Swinton.** *Derek Penney*

Bottom: **Recently reallocated from Westhouses (18B) MPD to Gorton (9G) 'Austerity' 2-8-0 No 90010 heads a steel coil train north of Lancaster in July 1962. No 90010 was to remain working from Gorton until withdrawn from traffic in February 1965.** *Derek Penney*

Above: **White-out conditions prevail on the Settle & Carlisle as BR/Sulzer Type 2 No D5186 passes through the cutting north of Dent station with a Skipton to Carlisle freight on 15 February 1969. The station at Dent is reached by a crazy corkscrew road which climbs 450ft in little more than a mile and is often referred to as the Coal Road.**
Freddie Bullock

Below: **Carrying the new BR logo, corporate blue-liveried 'Peak' No D20 heads a fully fitted eastbound freight away from Hellifield in 1966. The new arrow symbol, standard 'house' colours and distinctive letter form were all launched as part of a facelift for BR at an exhibition which took place at the Design Centre in London during January 1965.** *Freddie Bullock*

Entering its last year in operation 'Jubilee' No 45562 *Alberta* heads north past Grayrigg with the 'Border Countryman' railtour on 25 February 1967. No 45562 was one of eight 'Jubilees' to have soldiered on into 1967 and became the last of the class to remain in service. *Peter J. Fitton*

10
Special Traffic

For the first decade of the 20th century the railway had a secure monopoly of excursion traffic and the volume of business generated from these excursions showed no sign of lessening. In 1901 it was possible to 'go on an excursion' from Blackpool itself. A regular day trip left Talbot Road station at 10.00am bound for Fleetwood. Upon arrival the paddle steamer *Lady Evelyn* conveyed its passengers to Barrow across Morecambe Bay where a train left Ramsden Dock taking the passengers to Windermere, arriving at 12.50pm. The entire outing cost just seven shillings (35p), arriving back at Talbot Road station at 8.47pm.

By 1914, the people of every large manufacturing town except Coventry could reach the sea, even in winter, in less than 3hr.

As in World War 1, railway excursions were suspended during World War 2. At the end of hostilities, the main lines once again became packed with trippers travelling to the coastal resorts, but this was to be no more than an Indian Summer. With the spread of the motor car and the take-off in air travel together with the truncation of the BR system the future for the excursion train was doomed. Whilst their profitability was always marginal, some were certainly run as loss leaders.

With the decline of excursion traffic during the 1950s and 1960s it was surprising that British Railways was remarkably willing to accommodate the wishes of charter train organisers. Businesses would frequently take their employees on works outings often over little-used routes, and cyclists and ramblers would use railways to travel into the countryside.

It was societies like the Railway Correspondence & Travel Society, the Stephenson Locomotive Society and the Locomotive Club of Great Britain that would devise excursions for their members, sometimes travelling over little-used freight-only lines with a number of different locomotives that had been brought hundreds of miles for the purpose. The Cambridge University Railway Society even devised trips where their members could drive a steam locomotive over a local branch line. Luckily the days out for the undergraduates were confined to a Sunday when there were no other services.

In today's harsh financial climate there are no longer sidings full of carriages kept solely for use on excursion traffic perhaps only being used for some 30 or 40 trips a year. Having said that, the 1980s saw a modest revival when a separate sub-sector of InterCity saw the introduction of privately owned trains for use in the charter business. Under the direction of David Ward the Special Trains sub-sector became a viable business with its own rakes of coaches which were kept in first-class condition. Its business was divided into three distinct areas: business charters, leisure charters and the haulage of privately owned stock.

The business charters offered a level of corporate hospitality and were often run in connection with a special event such as the introduction of a new car or the opening of a new building. These charters were once the greatest contributors to Special Trains' profits and were often first class only, offering passengers lunch, tea or dinner at their seats.

Special Trains owned sets of coaches which formed the basis of the leisure charters sector and provided a continuation of the traditional excursions run for working men's clubs, women's institute and railway societies. Another part of this business were the trains run in conjunction with race meetings such as Ascot and the Cheltenham Gold Cup. Finally there was the revival of the two- or three-day Luxury Land Cruises which took the passengers through beautiful scenery in total comfort.

The Special Trains sector comprised 13 sets of stock, painted in InterCity livery with the exception of the steam set for the Fort William–Mallaig line which was kept in LNER excursion livery. The unit also had an allocation of 14 locomotives including the two that were set aside for Royal Train duties. In addition to these locomotives the unit would hire in an engine from one of the freight sectors to meet a special request from a railway society. The train crew was made up of a chief steward, two chefs as well as volunteers from InterCity Onboard Services. There were also the services of train managers and hostesses to ensure the smooth running of the train or any problems that arose from late running, such as missed connections home.

Above: **Organised by the South Bedfordshire Loco Club, the 'Banburian' railtour is captured entering Luton Bute Street behind LNWR 'Super D' 0-8-0 No 48930 on 22 September 1962. These locomotives could be heard miles away with their 'two-loud-then-two-gentle' exhaust beats with the second of the loud beats noticeably louder than the first.** *John Carter*

Below: **This picture taken on 13 October 1963 depicts Fowler 'Crab' 2-6-0 No 42896 at Lichfield Trent Valley's high level platform. This railway enthusiast tour organised by Vic Forster of the Railway Correspondence & Travel Society began in Nottingham and continued via Crewe to its final destination at Horwich Works.** *Ken Fairey*

Left: The scene at Aintree Sefton Arms station on Grand National Day, 8 April 1972, as Brush-Sulzer Type 4 No 1618 prepares to leave with 1L03, a race day special returning to London Euston. This locomotive has carried the numbers 47037, 47563, 47831, the name *Bolton Wanderer* and is still operational today as Virgin Thunderbird recovery locomotive No 57310 *Kyrano*. *Peter J. Fitton*

Left: The Grand National Day scene on 31 March 1962. Here Walton on the Hill (27E) MPD's Fowler 0-6-0 No 43988 is acting as station pilot at Aintree Central and is heading ecs which will form a return special to Cleethorpes. The observation car, M280M, built for the SR's 'Devon Belle' and dating from 1947, was transferred to the LMR in the mid-1950s. *Peter J. Fitton*

Below: In splendid Lake District scenery on the Cockermouth, Keswick & Penrith Railway, English Electric Type 4 No D313 pilots Carlisle Kingmoor (12A) MPD's Ivatt Class 4 2-6-0 No 43139 near Troutbeck with a returning Keswick Convention special train to London Euston on 22 July 1967. *Peter J. Fitton*

Above: **An interesting picture taken on the southern climb to Shap summit on 26 September 1964 as pink-liveried Brush-Sulzer Type 4 No D1624 has charge of the Crewe Works 'running-in' train consisting of almost life-expired ex-LMS stock — a challenge for the model maker?** *T. B. Owen*

Below: **Restored for use on enthusiast specials, former Caledonian Railway 4-2-2 No 123 and ex-Great North of Scotland Railway 4-4-0 No 49 *Gordon Highlander* are passing Kirkbride with an RCTS railtour on the Carlisle to Silloth branch on 13 June 1964.** *N. Fields*